Threads of Revelation Series

DAWN OF ETERNITY
EDENS LEGACY UNRAVELED

PAT DENIM

Reviews are important to independent authors, so if you have the time, I would really appreciate you leaving one for this book. Thank you.

Pat Denim

Threads of Revelation Series

DAWN OF ETERNITY:
EDENS LEGACY UNRAVELED

Cover Design by: P. Denim

Table of Contents

Explore the origins of heaven and earth,
Where divine breath gives life its worth.
In poetic prose, behold the splendor,
As worlds are shaped with divine candor.

Witness the dawn of humanity's birth,
Adam and Eve, a garden of infinite worth.
But temptation looms, a serpent's deceit,
Leading to a fall, a bitter retreat.

From Cain's envy to Noah's ark,
Genesis weaves tales both light and dark.
A flood's cleansing, a covenant's embrace,
Divine mercy shining through in every case.

Through the patriarchs' lineage, a promise is made,
Abraham, Isaac, Jacob, their destinies laid.
Dreams and visions, wrestling with the divine,
Unfolding the tapestry of a chosen bloodline.

Amidst trials and tests, faith perseveres,
Joseph's rise, a tale of hopes and fears.
From the pit to the palace, his journey unfolds,
A testament to dreams and destiny foretold.

This eBook invites you to journey back in time,
To immerse yourself in Genesis, sublime.
Let its poetic verses ignite your imagination,
Revealing ancient truths and divine revelation.

Discover the power of creation's song,
And the human spirit, resilient and strong.
Genesis, an epic of beginnings and strife,
A testament to the tapestry of human life.

LIFE'S GENESIS

The world began with God's creation,
Heavens, earth, void - the foundation.
Darkness covered the deep, no light in sight,
Yet the Spirit of God moved with delight.

The Spirit of God hovered near,
Over the waters, devoid of cheer.
And then God spoke, "Let there be light!"
And light appeared, banishing the night.

The light was good, so God did part,
Separating light from the dark in His heart.
Day and night were born, evening and morn,
Thus the first day of creation was born.

On the second day, God did decree,
An expanse in the midst of the sea.
Heavens were formed, waters divided,
Thus the second day was provided.

Third day came, and God said then,
"Let the waters gather, dry land begin"
God spoke, and plants came forth to bear,
Fruits and seeds, all with great care.

On day four, God created the light,
The sun, moon, and stars shining bright,
To separate day from night, and be a guide,
God's work, majestic and flawless worldwide.

The fifth day, the waters brought forth,
Living creatures, fish, and birds of worth,
God blessed them to multiply and thrive,
To fill the waters and the skies.

The sixth day came, and the land was alive,
With cattle, beasts, and creeping things, to thrive,
Humans were made, in God's image, the plan,
To rule over all, and to care for this land.

God blessed them, with fruitful way,
Multiply and fill, with love each day.
All plants for food, to man He gave,
And all creatures, the earth to save.

God saw all He made, and it was good,
Creation complete, the way it should.
The evening and the morning, six days done,
God's creation, a masterpiece, second to none.

EDEN'S HARMONY

The heavens and the earth were done,
With all their lights, God's work was won.
On the seventh day He rested well,
From all His work that He did excel.

God blessed and sanctified that day,
For all His work in a perfect way.
No shrub or plant was on the land,
No rain had fallen, no human hand.

A mist would water the ground,
And make the whole earth's surface sound.
From dust, God made a living soul,
Breathed life into it, to make it whole.

A garden in Eden God did plant,
Where He placed the man He did enchant.
Trees of every kind did grow,
And a river out of Eden did flow.

Four rivers from that one did divide,
The land with gold and stones supplied.
God put the man in the garden to care,
And commanded him, what to eat and beware.

Man could not be alone, God knew,
He created a partner, with love, so true,
Every animal He brought to his aid,
But none were right, none would he trade.

So from man's rib, God formed a woman,
And together they were one, in love, human,
They were naked, but not ashamed,
In the garden, where they remained.

THE BLAME GAME

In the garden, the serpent spoke
To Eve, and her resolve was broke
"Did God really say you can't eat?
From every tree, a single treat?"

Eve replied, "We may eat with ease,
From every tree, except one of these,
In the middle stands a tree so fair,
Touch or eat, we must not dare."

The serpent said, "You won't surely die,
Your eyes will open, and you'll be wise,
You'll be like God, knowing good and evil,
Take a bite, and your life will be delightful."

Seeing the fruit was good to taste,
Eve and Adam both took in haste,
Eating the fruit, their eyes revealed,
Naked they were, so they quickly concealed.

Their eyes were opened, and they knew,
That they were naked, exposed to view,
They sewed fig leaves together. and hid in fear,
"Where are you?" God called, their shame was clear.

He asked, "Have you eaten of the tree,
I told you not to, can't you see?"
Adam blamed Eve, Eve blamed the snake,
Consequences came with each mistake.

God then turned to the woman, and asked,
"What have you done?" She replied, unmasked,
"The serpent deceived me, and I ate,
I'm sorry Lord, please don't berate."

Cursed by God, the serpent's fate was sealed,
Made to slither and crawl, his body revealed,
Eating dust, despised by all around,
Enemies forever, with the woman he found.

God then spoke to Eve, and said,
"Childbirth will bring you pain, ahead,
Though childbirth shall be filled with strife,
Your husband shall govern you all your life.

To Adam, God then made it clear,
Cursed is the ground, for all the year,
Thorns and thistles, your work will spoil,
Until you return to dust, and end your toil.

God worked swiftly, crafting clothes of skin,
For Adam and Eve, who stood there in chagrin.
No longer could they stay in Eden's embrace,
Their hearts heavy, their souls in disgrace.

Guarded by cherubim and a flaming sword,
They journeyed outward, in one accord.
Their hope in God's mercy, their trust in His love,
Guided by His hand, to the promise above.

FIRSTBORN'S ENVY

In ancient times, the story goes,
A man named Adam and his wife, chose
To start a family of their own,
And soon, their firstborn son was known.

Eve gave birth to Cain, a boy,
And with the Lord's help, she felt great joy.
Then, Abel came, his brother dear,
A keeper of flocks, with nothing to fear.

Cain worked the ground and brought an offering,
But Abel's gift was much more pleasing.
Cain's jealousy consumed his heart
And he rose against Abel, tore him apart..

God asked Cain, "Where's your brother, dear?"
Cain replied, "I don't know, do I have to fear?"
God said, "Your brother's blood cries out to Me
You'll be cursed and the ground won't yield to thee."

Cain said, "My punishment's too great to bear
I'll be a wanderer, lost and nowhere to care"
But God marked him to keep him safe from harm
And Cain wandered east, far from his farm.

Cain and his wife then bore a son
And built a city, naming it after their firstborn one
Their descendants brought forth more sons
And the family tree grew, bearing fruitful ones..

Lamech, a descendant of Cain, spoke loud
Boasting about killing men with pride endowed
But God provided a son to Adam and Eve
Seth was his name, a new hope to receive..

Enosh, Seth's son, was the beginning
Of people calling on the Lord and singing
Through the generations, His name was proclaimed
As humanity grew, in God's image framed.

THE FIRST GENERATION

In the beginning, Adam was made
In God's likeness, he was portrayed
Male and female, both created
And "mankind" was their name, celebrated.

At one hundred and thirty years
Adam fathered Seth, a son so dear
Eight hundred years he lived and more
Sons and daughters he did adore..

Seth, at one hundred and five
Fathered Enosh, his legacy alive
Eight hundred and seven years he lived
His family, with love, he did give.

Enosh, ninety years, did father Kenan
He lived eight hundred and fifteen, then
Sons and daughters, he did beget
Family ties, he'd never forget.

Seventy years, Kenan, lived and breathed
Mahalalel, his son, he did bequeath
Eight hundred and forty years he did live
His love and guidance, he did give.

Mahalalel, at sixty-five
Fathered Jared, to keep his name alive
Eight hundred and thirty years he did survive
His love for family, he did strive.

At one hundred and sixty-two
Jared, Enoch's father, was true
Eight hundred years, he lived and more
Sons and daughters, he did adore

Enoch, at sixty-five, had Methuselah born
Three hundred years with God, he did adorn
Sons and daughters, he did rear
With God, he did draw near

Methuselah, one hundred eighty-seven
Lived and fathered Lamech in heaven
Seven hundred eighty-two years he did live
His family, his all, he did give

Lamech, one hundred eighty-two
Fathered Noah, a son so true
His comfort from labor, he did proclaim
His family, he did sustain

At five hundred years, Noah did rise
Father of Shem, Ham, and Japheth, wise
This book of generations, a story to tell
Of family ties, and love, they did excel.

DELUGE

In the days of old, when man was new
And daughters born, to a world askew
Sons of God saw their beauty fair
And took them as wives, without a care

But the Lord looked down with a heavy heart
For man's wickedness tore him apart
"My spirit cannot stay," He said
"Man's days on earth will soon be dead"

Nephilim walked the land and sea
Born from the union of God and humanity
Mighty men, of old renown
Yet their fate, soon to be down

For the Lord saw man's evil ways
And decided to end their numbered days
"I'll wipe them out," He said with might
"And animals and crawling things in sight"

But Noah found favor in God's eyes
A righteous man, blameless and wise
He walked with God and followed His plan
To build an ark and save his clan

The earth was corrupt and filled with strife
Violence, a part of everyday life
God said to Noah, "It's the end for man
I'll destroy them all, as part of my plan"

"Build an ark of gopher wood," He said
"Cover it in pitch, and make it your bed
300 cubits in length, 30 in height and 50 in width,
To weather the flood's wrathful hit"

"Bring two of every kind," God commanded
"Male and female, by your hand they'll be stranded
Food for you and them, you'll need to gather
For this flood, nothing will matter"

So Noah did as God did say
And prepared for the coming day
He saved his family and every kind
For God's covenant with him to bind.

A WORLD SUBMERGED

Noah and his family were righteous,
In a world filled with sin and vices.
God spoke to him, said to build an ark,
For a great flood was soon to embark.

Clean animals were to come in seven pairs,
While unclean ones came only in twos and pairs.
Birds of the sky also came in seven,
So that they may survive and thrive in heaven.

Rain would fall for forty days and nights,
Destroying everything in its might.
So Noah obeyed the Lord's command,
And followed through with His demand.

As the waters rose, the ark did too,
Floating on the surface, as if on cue.
The mountains were covered, the earth submerged,
All creatures on it, no longer emerged.

For 150 days, the waters prevailed,
And every living thing was derailed.
But Noah and his family, they were saved,
As they followed God's plan and behaved.

THE DOVE'S JOURNEY

God remembered Noah and the ark,
And all the creatures, day and dark.
A wind passed over, water went down,
Fountains and floodgates closed all around.

For 150 days, the water decreased,
And on mountains of Ararat, the ark was released.
By the tenth month, mountain tops were seen,
And after forty days, a raven flew the scene.

The raven flew here and there,
Until the water subsided everywhere.
Then Noah sent out a dove,
But it found no resting place above.

The dove returned to the ark,
No place to land in the water so dark.
After seven days, Noah sent it out again,
And in its beak, an olive leaf he did gain.

Seven more days, he sent the dove out,
But this time, it did not return about.
The water had dried up from the earth,
Noah removed the covering, felt rebirth.

On the twenty-seventh day, the earth was dry,
God spoke to Noah, it was time to say goodbye.
He and his family, and creatures, too,
Left the ark to start anew.

Noah built an altar, offerings to make,
The Lord was pleased with the sweet scent to take.
He promised never to curse the ground,
And never again to destroy all around.

"While the earth remains," God said,
"Seed time and harvest, cold and heat ahead,
Summer and winter, day and night,
Shall not cease, everything will be alright."

COVENANT OF THE RAINBOW

God blessed Noah and his sons,
And said to them, "Fill the earth,
Multiply and be fruitful,
All creatures will fear your worth.

Every animal, every bird,
All that crawls and swims the sea,
Are handed over to you,
As I gave the green plant, for free.

You may eat all moving things,
As food, as I have given,
But do not consume flesh with blood,
For it is sacred, not for living.

For every lifeblood I will require,
From animals and from man,
For shedding human blood, you shall pay,
In the image of God, you stand.

Be fruitful, multiply, and spread,
Abundantly populate the earth,
For I am making a covenant with you,
And with all creatures, for all future birth.

All flesh shall never again be eliminated,
By waters of a flood, that once destroyed,
The rainbow in the cloud shall serve as a sign,
Of the everlasting covenant, I have employed.

Noah's sons came out of the ark,
And populated the whole earth,
Noah began farming, planted a vineyard,
But became drunk, a moment of dearth.

Ham saw his father's nakedness,
But Shem and Japheth covered it with grace,
Noah cursed Ham's son, Canaan,
But blessed God and Shem's embrace.

Noah lived for 350 years,
After the flood had passed,
All the days of Noah were 950,
Till his last breath, the legacy had amassed.

DIVIDED NATIONS

These are the generations of Noah's kin
Sons of Shem, Ham, and Japheth within
After the flood, they were born anew
Their lines divided, their tongues askew

From Japheth came Gomer, Tubal, and more
Elishah, Tarshish, and Kittim before
Coastlands separated by their clan
Distinct nations formed by God's own hand

Ham's sons were Cush, Put, and Mizraim too
Their lines spread far, their tribes anew
Nimrod, a mighty hunter, he became
His rule began in Babel, his fame

Mizraim's kin Ludim and Philistines bred
Caphtorim and Pathrusim, their lines led
Canaan's firstborn was Sidon, it's told
His brothers spread wide, their tribes enrolled

Shem's sons were Elam, Lud, and more
Arpachshad fathered Eber, he bore
Two sons, Peleg and Joktan, they grew
Joktan's sons settled eastward, it's true

These are the families of Noah's kin
Descendants spread out, new nations begin
Their languages and lands, all unique
Divine plan fulfilled, God's will complete.

BABEL'S UNFINISHED TOWER

In a time long ago, all spoke as one
With the same language and the same tongue
As they journeyed east, they found a plain
In Shinar they settled and decided to remain

"Come," they said, "let us make bricks and fire
Use tar for mortar, let our city reach higher
Let us build a tower to the heavens above
Make a name for ourselves, show our love"

But the LORD saw their deeds and spoke with concern
"All have the same language, what will they learn?
Nothing will be impossible for them to do
Let us confuse their speech, and their plans undo"

So the LORD scattered them across the land
The city unfinished, they could not understand
Babel they named it, where their language was lost
And from there, they spread at an immeasurable cost

These are the generations of Shem, son of Noah
Fathered Arpachshad, and many more to show for
Each one lived for hundreds of years, it seems
With sons and daughters, fulfilling their dreams

Terah fathered Abram, Nahor, and Haran
Haran died in Ur, the place of their clan
Abram married Sarai, and Nahor wed Milcah
But Sarai could not conceive, it was her flaw

Terah, with his family, departed from Ur
To go to Canaan, a new life to explore
They settled in Haran, where Terah died
Leaving Abram to continue with God as his guide.

FAMINE AND FLIGHT

The Lord spoke to Abram,
"Leave your land and kin,
Depart from your father's house,
And go where I will begin.

I'll make you a great nation,
Your name will be renowned,
A blessing to all around,
And in you, families will be crowned.

Those who bless you, I'll bless,
And those who curse, I'll curse too,
So Abram left as God had said,
With all that he knew.

With Sarai and Lot by his side,
And all they had acquired,
They set out for Canaan,
With faith and hope inspired.

Along the way, the Lord appeared,
And promised Abram's heirs,
This land would be their heritage,
A promise beyond compare.

But famine struck the land,
And to Egypt they had to flee,
Abram feared for Sarai's beauty,
And begged her to help him see.

He asked her to pretend,
To be his sister, not his wife,
And Pharaoh took her to his home,
Unaware of Abram's strife.

But the Lord struck Pharaoh,
With plagues for taking Sarai,
And Abram was forced to leave,
With all he had to rely.

Pharaoh returned Sarai,
And commanded Abram to go,
And so he left with all he owned,
With faith in God to show."

ALTAR OF DEDICATION

Abram's journey led him to the Negev,
With all he owned, including Lot, his kin.
His wealth in flocks and gold was truly great,
And on his journey he did contemplate.

He traveled far, from south to Bethel's gate,
To the altar he had made, to pray and meditate.
Lot had flocks and herds, and so did he,
Their possessions too much for them to agree.

Their herdsmen quarreled, their land too small,
And in the midst of it all, they stood tall.
Abram said to Lot, "Let's not fight,
We are family, let's separate and do what's right."

Lot chose the fertile Jordan land,
Like the garden of the Lord, it was grand.
Abram stayed in Canaan, as God commanded,
Lot moved to Sodom, where sin was expanded.

God spoke to Abram and said, "Look around,
All this land will be yours, forever bound.
Your descendants will be countless, like the dust,
And I will give it to you, without a fuss."

Abram moved to Hebron, by the oaks of Mamre,
And built an altar to the Lord, a place to share.
His journey was long, but God's promise was true,
For Abram and his descendants, the land was anew.

KINGS IN BATTLE

In the days of old kings four,
They made war and brought a roar,
With Bera and Birsha they fought,
And Shinab and Shemeber they sought.

Twelve years of service they gave,
To Chedorlaomer, strong and brave,
But in the thirteenth year they rebelled,
Their own kingdoms they upheld.

Chedorlaomer and his kings came,
And defeated the Rephaim in their game,
The Zuzim in Ham they overcame,
And the Emim in Shaveh-kiriathaim.

Mount Seir's Horites too they beat,
As far as El-paran, with their fleet,
Then they conquered the Amalekites,
And the Amorites with their might.

Sodom and Gomorrah's kings five,
In the Valley of Siddim did arrive,
Against the four kings who had won,
But into tar pits they had gone.

Abram's nephew Lot was taken,
And his possessions too, all forsaken,
But Abram, with his trained men strong,
Pursued them all night long.

He divided his forces, and defeated them,
And brought back all the possessions then,
And Lot and the women he had saved,
All the captives he had braved.

Melchizedek, king of Salem, brought bread,
And wine for Abram, who he led,
He blessed him, and said with awe,
"Blessed be Abram of God Most High."

"Blessed be Possessor of heaven and earth,
God Most High, who granted you worth."
Abram refused the king of Sodom's plea,
"I have sworn to the Lord, I will not take from thee."

"I will take nothing, except what we have eaten,
The share of Aner, Eshcol, and Mamre, with caution,"
So he returned home with his men,
And Lot and his possessions, safe again.

LAND OF MANY TRIBES

The word of the Lord to Abram came,
In a vision, bright and clear.
"Do not fear, Abram, for I am with you,
As a shield, I am always here.

Your reward shall be very great,"
The Lord said to Abram so kind.
But Abram asked, "What can you give,
When I am childless in mind?"

"My heir is Eliezer of Damascus,
Since no son has come from me."
The Lord replied, "From your own body,
An heir will come, wait and see.

Look at the stars in the sky,
Count them if you're able to.
Your descendants will be like them,
As many as the stars that you view."

Abram believed in the Lord,
And his faith was counted as right.
The Lord promised him this land,
To possess it with all his might.

But Abram asked, "Lord, how can I know
That I will truly possess it?"
"Bring me a heifer, goat, and ram,
And a turtledove and pigeon," the Lord did admit.

Abram brought them all and cut them in two,
Laid each half opposite the other.
The birds of prey came down to feast,
But Abram chased them away like a brother.

As the sun set, terror and darkness fell,
But the Lord spoke to Abram so true.
"Your descendants will be enslaved,
For four hundred years, it's true.

They'll be strangers in a foreign land,
But I will judge the nation they serve.
Afterward, they'll come out with many possessions,
And to this land, they'll return with nerve."

The Lord made a covenant with Abram that day,
To give his descendants this land so grand.
From the river of Egypt to the Euphrates,
The land of many tribes at hand.

WILD DONKEY OF A MAN

Sarai was barren, no child in sight,
But a slave woman, Hagar, was in her right,
She told Abram, "Take her to bed,
Perhaps a child can be conceived," she said.

So Abram agreed, and Hagar became his wife,
She bore his child, the joy of new life,
But Sarai felt insignificant and small,
Her slave woman now had it all.

Sarai blamed Abram for her pain,
Putting Hagar in his arms was her bane,
She said, "May the Lord judge you and me,
For the wrong done, let it be upon thee."

Abram replied, "She's in your power,
Do what you will, this is your hour."
So Sarai treated her slave harshly,
And Hagar fled, hurt and lonely.

In the wilderness, Hagar wept,
The angel of the Lord appeared and kept,
He told her to go back to her mistress' care,
And promised her a son, beyond compare.

"His name shall be Ishmael," the angel said,
"God heard your affliction, don't be afraid,
He'll be a wild donkey of a man,
Defiant, against all his brothers' clan."

Hagar praised the Lord who saw her pain,
And named the well, "Beer-lahai-roi," her gain,
She bore a son, Abram named him Ishmael,
At the age of eighty-six, his father could tell.

CIRCUMCISION

At ninety-nine years old, Abram heard
The voice of God, with solemn word
"I am God Almighty," said the Lord
"Walk blameless before Me, in accord

I'll make a covenant with you,
And multiply your offspring too"
Abram fell down, his face to ground
God spoke to him, His plan unbound

"My covenant is with you alone
Father of many nations, known
No longer Abram, but Abraham
Your name shall be, your legacy grand"

Kings will come from your own kin
Nations will rise, as you begin
My covenant with your descendants true
Everlasting, to always renew.

The land of Canaan, I will give
To your descendants, where they'll live
Circumcision, a sign of our pact
For all males, a holy act

As for Sarah, your wife dear
Her name will change, have no fear
She'll bear you a son, Isaac named
An everlasting covenant proclaimed

Ishmael, too, will be blessed
Father of twelve, his name confessed
But Isaac, your son, will fulfill
My covenant, with him, it will instill"

Abraham listened, his heart full
Circumcised himself, and his kin, in full
His covenant with God, forever sealed
As their faith and obedience revealed.

THE PROMISED SON

Under the oaks of Mamre,
On a hot and sunny day,
Abraham sat at his tent door,
W.hen three men came his way.

He bowed to them in respect,
And asked if they'd stay a while,
He offered them some water,
And bread to make them smile.

He rushed to prepare a feast,
For his honored guests to eat,
And the men spoke of a son,
That Sarah soon would meet.

Sarah laughed in disbelief,
But the Lord had a plan in mind,
Abraham begged for Sodom,
And pleaded for the divine.

He asked the Lord to spare,
For the sake of righteous men,
And the Lord agreed to save,
If even ten could be found within.

Abraham's faith was unwavering,
As he pleaded for the lives of many,
And the Lord departed from him,
Leaving Abraham with blessings plenty.

PILLAR OF SALT

The angels came to Sodom's town,
Lot saw them and he bowed down,
He urged them to his house to stay,
But they refused and went their way.

Lot begged them to come inside,
He baked some bread and then they dined,
But then men from the city came,
Demanding the angels bring them out in shame.

Lot pleaded for them to spare,
But they said it was not fair,
They tried to break down Lot's door,
But the angels struck them blind before.

The angels told Lot to escape,
Take his wife and daughters to a safe place,
But Lot hesitated to depart,
So the angels took hold of his hand and heart.

They led him out of the city's fate,
And warned him not to look back, it's too late,
The Lord rained fire on Sodom and Gomorrah's ground,
Lot's wife looked back and a pillar of salt, was found.

Abraham saw the smoke arise,
Of Sodom and Gomorrah, now destroyed, despised,
God saved Lot from the destruction's grip,
And he fled with his daughters to the mountains' tip.

THE RETURN OF SARAH

From the land he came
Towards Negev, his aim
Settling between Kadesh and Shur
For a time in Gerar, he'd endure

His wife, Sarah, he called his kin
A lie, that brought on a sin
Abimelech took her as his own
But in a dream, God made it known

Abimelech, a dead man he'd be
For taking Abraham's wife, the key
But blameless, he pled with God
For he knew not, the truth untold

In the integrity of his heart
He was saved, set apart
From sinning against the Lord
By the grace, he was assured

Abimelech returned Sarah to her man
And a thousand pieces of silver he ran
As vindication for Sarah's name
Her honor, in the eyes of all, reclaimed

Abraham prayed, and God made way
For Abimelech and his wife to have a say
Children they bore, as the Lord had planned
For Sarah, a special one, in God's hand.

DISPUTE OVER A WELL

The Lord remembered Sarah, as He had said,
And kept His promise, as He had pledged,
And Sarah conceived and bore a son,
To Abraham, in his old age, as God had done.

Isaac was his name, a joy to behold,
Abraham circumcised him, as God had foretold,
And Sarah said, "God has made laughter for me,
Everyone who hears will laugh with me."

But trouble brewed when Hagar's son
Mocked Isaac, Sarah's only one,
She demanded they be cast away,
Abraham was distressed, but God had His say.

"Do as Sarah says, listen to her voice,
Through Isaac, your descendants will rejoice,
But Hagar's son, fear not for he will thrive,
I will make a nation of his line to survive."

So Abraham gave bread and water to Hagar,
And sent her and her son, to the wilderness afar,
But when the water was used up, she cried,
God heard the boy, and an angel arrived.

"What is the matter with you, Hagar?" he said,
"Do not fear, God has heard your son's cry ahead,
Take him up, for a great nation he'll be,
And God opened her eyes, a well of water to see.

Ishmael grew and lived in the wilderness,
He became an archer, a man of great prowess,
And his mother found him a wife from Egypt's land,
As they lived on, in the desert's hot sand.

Abimelech and Phicol came to Abraham,
And said, "God is with you, a great man",
They made a covenant to be true,
Abraham complained of a well taken, too.

Abimelech denied knowledge of the deed,
So Abraham gave sheep and oxen in need,
And seven ewe lambs to seal the deal,
At Beersheba, they made an oath to seal.

Abraham planted a tamarisk tree,
And called on the Lord, the Everlasting to see,
And he resided in Philistine's land,
For many days, a life of peace and grand.

PREPARING THE SACRIFICE

God spoke to Abraham one day
And asked him to obey
To take his son, his precious son
And offer him as a burnt offering

Without question, Abraham rose
He took his son and two young men, chose
Split wood for the offering
And journeyed to the place God was directing

After three days, they reached the site
Abraham built an altar and placed it right
Bound his son on top of the wood
And raised his knife as he thought he should

Then the angel of the Lord called out
To Abraham, to stop and doubt
"Do not harm the boy," the angel said
"For I know now, you fear and obey."

Abraham looked around and found
A ram with its horns caught in the ground
And offered it instead of his son
And named the place where it was done

The Lord said to Abraham, "Because of this act
Your descendants will be blessed, that's a fact
As many as the stars in the sky
Your seed will multiply."

And so, Abraham returned home
With his son and young men alone
Knowing he had passed the test
And that God's promises will manifest.

PURCHASE OF THE CAVE

Sarah, at 127 years old,
In Hebron, Canaan, left the fold.
Abraham, in mourning, came to weep,
For his beloved, now at eternal sleep.

He spoke to the sons of Heth, he said,
"I am a foreigner, among the dead.
Grant me a place to lay her to rest,
A burial site, where she'll be blessed."

The sons of Heth, they did reply,
"Your request, my lord, we won't deny.
Bury your dead in our choicest of graves,
A place where she'll forever be saved."

Abraham then bowed to the land's people,
If they'd let him bury, it would be so simple.
"Please plead with Ephron, I implore,
To sell me the cave, to be hers forevermore."

Ephron sat among the sons of Heth,
To Abraham, he spoke with a kind breath,
"I'll give you the field, and the cave within,
A place where your loved one can begin."

But Abraham insisted on paying the price,
He weighed out four hundred shekels precise.
The field, the cave, and all within,
Deeded to Abraham, in front of all men.

And so, Sarah was laid to rest,
In the field of Machpelah, where she'll be blessed.
A burial site, deeded over to Abraham,
By the sons of Heth, in the land of Canaan.

CHOSEN MATCH

Abraham, old and blessed by God,
Spoke to his trusted servant, tasked to nod:
"Place your hand beneath my thigh,
Swear to God above, don't even try

To take a Canaanite wife for Isaac,
To my country and kin, go and find a match."
The servant questioned, "What if she won't come?
Shall I bring Isaac to that distant home?"

Abraham replied, "Beware and listen well,
Do not take my son there, no, never tell
The Lord will send His angel to guide
You to the right woman, do not be denied

But if she refuses, release the oath
Leave my son in peace, that's what I'm told."
The servant swore and set out with ten camels,
To Nahor he went, with gifts and ample

Praying to the Lord for success and aid
That a woman with kindness he'd find and braid.
At the well, Rebekah appeared like fate,
Beautiful and virgin, ready to date

The servant asked for a sip from her jar
She graciously gave, a sign from afar
He asked whose daughter, she answered, "Bethuel's,
Son of Nahor, with plenty of room to dwell."

Overwhelmed, the servant gave gifts of gold,
Ten shekels of bracelets, a ring to behold.
He inquired about lodgings, she welcomed with glee
The man bowed and thanked the Lord in jubilee.

Rebekah's brother Laban then appeared
He invited the servant, as he neared
To come into their home and rest with the crew,
And there they were welcomed and dined on stew.

BIRTHRIGHT BETRAYAL

Abraham took Keturah for his wife,
And they had six sons to bring to life.
Zimran, Jokshan, Medan, Midian,
Ishbak, and Shuah, all their kin.

Jokshan fathered Sheba and Dedan,
Asshurim, Letushim, and Leummim came.
Midian had Ephah, Epher, Hanoch,
Abida, and Eldaah, sons to watch.

All Abraham had, to Isaac he gave,
But his concubines' sons, he did not save.
He gave them gifts and sent them away,
To the land of the east, to live and stay.

Abraham lived 175 years,
Satisfied with life, free from fears.
He died and was buried with Sarah,
By his sons Isaac and Ishmael's care.

Isaac was blessed by God on high,
And he lived by Beer-lahai-roi.
The records of Ishmael's sons,
Twelve princes with their camps and homes.

Isaac married Rebekah, the Aramean,
She could not bear children, causing pain.
But the Lord heard Isaac's plea,
And Rebekah conceived, soon to see.

She gave birth to twins, a struggle within,
Two nations to come, one to win.
Esau came out red and hairy,
Jacob held his heel, name to carry.

Esau was a hunter, skilled and strong,
Jacob, civilized, loved by his mom.
Esau sold his birthright for a stew,
And despised it, as Jacob knew.

RECONCILIATION

Isaac, son of Abraham, in famine was caught,
So he went to Gerar where Philistines wrought.
The Lord said to stay, in Egypt do not roam,
In this land live, and I'll bless you with a home.

All these lands I'll give to your seed and you,
As stars of heaven, your offspring will be too.
Nations of the earth will also be blessed,
For Abraham obeyed and did pass the test.

Isaac lived in Gerar, men asked of his wife,
He said, "She's my sister," fearing for his life.
After some time, King Abimelech spied,
Isaac and Rebekah, with love in their eyes.

Abimelech said, "She is truly your wife,
Why did you lie, putting us at strife?"
Isaac said, "I feared someone would kill,
Me for her beauty, but now I'll be still."

Abimelech commanded, "No one should touch,
This man and his wife, or they'll suffer much."
Isaac sowed and reaped a hundred times more,
The Lord blessed him and his wealth did soar.

Philistines were jealous, filled wells with dirt,
So Isaac moved on to a new spot to assert.
He dug the wells his father Abraham had,
And gave them the same names, which made him glad.

The first was Esek, meaning "contention,"
The second, Sitnah, for strife's prevention.
Third was Rehoboth, "Now the Lord has made room,"
Isaac was grateful and felt like a boom.

He went up to Beersheba and pitched his tent,
Built an altar to God, where he bent.
The Lord appeared to him and made a decree,
"Blessed you'll be, for the sake of Abraham's legacy."

Abimelech saw that Isaac was blessed,
So he came to make peace, and be addressed.
They made a covenant to do no harm,
Exchanged oaths, and left with much calm.

THE RIVALRY OF BROTHERS

Isaac was old, his eyes were dim,
He called for Esau, his son, so prim.
"My son," he said, "please hear my plea,
I do not know when death will come for me.

Take your gear, your bow, and your quiver,
And hunt some game so that I may deliver,
A meal delicious and savory,
Before my soul departs from me.

Rebekah listened to Isaac's voice,
And heard him make his meal choice.
She told Jacob, "Your father asks,
For a tasty meal, a simple task.

Go to the flock, and fetch me goats,
Two young, and perfect, I'll prepare the roasts.
Bring them to me, so I can cook,
And your father's blessing you'll have took."

But Jacob, in fear, replied with doubt,
"Esau's hairy, and I'm smooth, no clout.
He'll know it's me and bring me curse,
Not a blessing, it will be worse."

Rebekah said, "Don't worry, my son,
Your father's blessing must be won.
Obey my voice, bring the goats to me,
And the blessing of your father you'll see."

Rebekah took Esau's best clothes,
Put them on Jacob, as her plan arose.
She put goat skins on his hands and neck,
To mimic Esau, who she would check.

Jacob approached his father with the meal,
And said, "I am Esau, it's my seal.
Eat my game so that you may bless,
Me before your final rest."

Isaac asked, "How did you get this game?
It was quick, it seems, almost tame."
Jacob replied, "God gave me this chance,
And I took it with swift advance."

Isaac felt Jacob's hands and said,
"The voice is Jacob's, but the skin is red.
Are you really my son, Esau?
Yes," said Jacob, "I am, it's no faux."

Isaac blessed Jacob with words of grace,
That he would rule in a favored place.
Esau came too late, the blessing was gone,
And he wept bitterly for what he'd done.

JACOB'S DREAM

Isaac to Jacob gave a command,
A wife from Canaan, he must not demand.
To Paddan-aram, he must depart,
And take a wife from Laban's heart.

May God Almighty bless your way,
Make you fruitful, and multiply each day.
A multitude of peoples, you shall be,
Blessed with Abraham's legacy.

Esau saw Jacob's blessings unfold,
And that he obeyed, as he was told.
Canaan's daughters Isaac did despise,
So Esau sought a wife in another guise.

Jacob set out from Beersheba's land,
Towards Haran, on his way to stand.
He chanced upon a place that night,
And dreamt of a ladder to God's sight.

The Lord said, "This land is yours to keep,
Your descendants will be many, as they sleep.
Spread out to the east, west, north, and south,
And all families of earth shall bless your mouth."

Jacob awoke, feeling amazed,
The Lord's presence, he had grazed.
Fear and awe, filled his heart,
This place was holy, and set apart.

Early morning, he set up a stone,
To remember this moment, when alone.
He poured oil on its top, and said a prayer,
This place, Bethel, now so rare.

He made a vow, to give a tenth,
Of all that he earned, God's love to augment.
If God kept him safe, on his journey's way,
The Lord would be his God, every day.

SEVEN-YEAR WAIT

Jacob set out on his journey,
To the land of the people of the east,
A well he saw in the field,
Where sheep gathered to drink and feast.

Three flocks were lying beside,
The stone on the well was large,
They would roll it away and provide,
Water to quench their thirst at large.

Jacob asked his brothers,
"Where are you from?"
They replied, "We are from Haran,
And know Laban, Nahor's son."

Rachel, Laban's daughter, approached,
With her father's sheep to tend,
Jacob rolled the stone and watered them,
Then kissed Rachel, his heart to mend.

Laban embraced Jacob as his kin,
Said, "Stay with me, you're bone and flesh,"
He offered wages for Jacob to begin,
And said, "I have two daughters, choose which."

Jacob loved Rachel and agreed,
To serve for seven years with zeal,
For her hand in marriage he plead,
To Laban, who made the deal.

On their wedding night,
Laban played a deceitful hand,
Leah was given to Jacob in sight,
Who had not planned this in his demand.

Laban explained his custom,
To marry off the elder first,
He gave Rachel to Jacob in turn,
For another seven years of thirst.

Leah bore Jacob sons,
Reuben, Simeon, and Levi,
Hoping her husband's love would come,
But Jacob's heart was with Rachel, so nigh.

Rachel, though, was barren,
But Leah bore her own share,
Judah, her fourth son was her token,
To praise the Lord in thanks and prayer.

Thus Jacob's journey began,
With deceit, love, and family ties,
A story of human struggle and plan,
Told through generations, it never dies.

LOVE, RIVALRY, AND MOTHERHOOD

Jealousy, a fire that burns bright,
Rachel's heart filled with spite,
Rachel's arms were left to yearn,
Leah's children came in turn.

Rachel begged Jacob for a child,
Her pain, her anguish, driving her wild,
But Jacob replied with anger,
"You ask too much, it's not in my power."

Desperate, Rachel offered her maid,
Bilhah, to Jacob, to conceive a babe,
And thus Dan, her son, was born,
Rachel rejoiced, her heart no longer torn.

Bilhah bore another son, Naphtali,
Rachel's victory over Leah, so sweet,
But Leah had a plan up her sleeve,
Her maid, Zilpah, to Jacob she would leave.

Zilpah bore Gad and then Asher,
And Leah's heart, happy and lighter,
But Rachel coveted Leah's son's fruit,
Mandrakes, a delicacy, so cute.

Rachel begged Leah, "Please, give me some,
Of your son's mandrakes, just one,"
But Leah refused, her heart full of strife,
"You want my husband, and now my son's life?"

But Rachel, persistent, made a deal,
To sleep with Jacob, her heart full of zeal,
And Leah's son's mandrakes were hers to keep,
A small price to pay, for Rachel's heart to leap.

Leah bore more sons, Issachar and Zebulun,
But Rachel, still childless, was undone,
Until God opened her womb at last,
Joseph, her son, born, her pain now past.

Jacob, with his wives and children in tow,
Wanted to leave, his own home to know,
But Laban, his father-in-law, begged him to stay,
Divining that God had blessed him in every way.

Jacob proposed a deal, to take the spotted sheep,
As his wages, his flock to keep,
Laban agreed, but tried to cheat,
Jacob outwitted him, his flocks he did beat.

Thus Jacob prospered, his family strong,
And Rachel, finally, her heart's desire long,
Children born, a family complete,
Her jealousy, her pain, now obsolete.

STOLEN IDOLS

Laban's Sons accused Jacob,
"Of stealing their father's wealth."
Laban's attitude turned unfriendly,
Making Jacob feel alone in stealth.

God spoke to Jacob and said,
"Return to your land and kin."
Jacob told Rachel and Leah,
God will protect us, let's begin.

Jacob reminded them how hard he worked,
For their father, who cheated him so.
God gave Jacob wealth and fortune,
When Laban's cheating he did show.

Jacob saw the male goats in a dream,
Striped, speckled, and mottled they were.
The angel of God said to Jacob,
"Leave this land, and return to where you were."

Rachel and Leah asked Jacob,
"Is there anything left for us here?"
Laban had sold them and consumed their wealth,
Their future with Jacob, without fear.

Jacob took his family and possessions,
Fleeing without Laban's knowledge.
He headed towards the hill country of Gilead,
While Laban pursued him, seeking vengeance.

God warned Laban, "Don't harm Jacob,"
In a dream, and he caught up with him.
"Why did you deceive and steal my gods?"
Laban asked, while his anger grew dim.

Jacob didn't know Rachel had stolen the idols,
But Laban searched and didn't find.
Rachel sat on them, hidden in a saddlebag,
Laban went back home, his heart unkind.

NIGHT OF WRESTLING

As Jacob journeyed on his way,
Angels of God appeared that day,
And Jacob knew he was in God's camp,
Thus Mahanaim was the place he named.

He sent messengers to Esau's land,
Instructing them with his command,
To tell his lord of his residence,
And to find favor in his presence.

But news came back that Esau and four hundred men,
Were on their way, causing fear to descend,
Jacob divided his people and flocks,
So if attacked, one group would escape the shocks.

He prayed to God, his fathers' Lord,
For protection, help, and reward,
He knew he was unworthy of all grace,
For he crossed Jordan with only his staff to trace.

That night he chose a gift for Esau,
Goats, ewes, camels, cows, and donkeys, without a flaw,
And sent them ahead, hoping to appease,
And then himself stayed back with unease.

As he crossed the Jabbok, he was left alone,
And a man appeared and wrestled with him to the bone,
Jacob held on and would not let go,
Until the man blessed him and his name did bestow.

His name was changed to Israel that day,
For he had contended with God and men in every way,
Jacob had seen the face of God in that fight,
And even though he limped, he emerged with new sight.

Thus, the sons of Israel do not eat,
The tendon of the hip, in honor of that defeat,
Jacob was spared his life that night,
And God's grace was his guiding light.

A PLACE TO CALL HOME

Jacob and Esau, brothers estranged,
400 men with Esau came.
Jacob, fearing for his family's fate,
Divided them in order, great.

He put the slave women first in line,
With their children, so meek and kind.
Then Leah and her children, next in queue,
And Rachel with Joseph, last to view.

Jacob bowed to the ground seven times,
Ahead of his family, they followed behind.
When Esau saw Jacob, he ran to meet,
And they hugged, and cried, and shared a seat.

Esau asked of the children and wives,
Jacob replied, "Gifts from God, our lives."
They all bowed down to show respect,
And Jacob gave a gift to Esau, a debt.

Esau offered to journey together,
But Jacob declined, for the weather.
The children and flocks could not keep pace,
Jacob would follow at a leisurely pace.

Jacob settled in Shechem, safe and sound,
He bought a plot of land, built a house, and found,
A place to worship, an altar for his God,
El-Elohe-Israel, a name he laud.

BLOODSHED IN THE CITY

Dinah's visit to see the land,
Led to a moment unplanned,
Shechem saw her and was smitten,
But his love was not befitting.

He took her and defiled her,
A heinous act to occur,
Though he loved her tenderly,
His actions were not friendly.

Shechem desired Dinah as his wife,
But her family was filled with strife,
For he had done a shameful thing,
Against the daughter of their king.

Hamor, Shechem's father, spoke,
His son's love was no joke,
He asked for Dinah's hand in marriage,
But it was met with angry disparage.

Jacob's sons wanted revenge,
Their sister's honor to avenge,
They proposed a deceitful plan,
Forcing circumcision upon the man.

Shechem agreed, and so did his father,
They thought the plan was clever,
But on the third day, Simeon and Levi,
Killed every man in the city.

They took their sister and all the loot,
Jacob feared retaliation, astute,
He scolded his sons for the trouble they brought,
But they replied, for Dinah they fought.

FAMILY LEGACY

God spoke to Jacob, calling him to rise,
To Bethel, where he should reside,
To build an altar and offer sacrifice,
To the God who had been his guide.

Jacob commanded his household and all,
To rid themselves of foreign gods,
And to purify and change before the call,
To make themselves right with the Lord.

As they traveled, fear fell on the cities around,
And they were not pursued by any foe,
Jacob and his people finally found,
Their way to Bethel, where they would go.

There, Jacob built an altar to God above,
And named the place El-bethel, for the sight,
Where God had revealed Himself in love,
When Jacob fled from his brother's might.

God appeared to Jacob once again,
Blessing him with a new name,
No longer would he be known as Jacob then,
But Israel, with a new claim to fame.

God promised Jacob a great legacy,
A nation and kings from his line would come,
The land he had given to Abraham and Isaac previously,
Would now be given to Jacob's own.

Rachel, Jacob's beloved wife, passed away,
And was buried on the way to Bethlehem,
A memorial stone Jacob did lay,
To honor her memory, he did then.

Isaac, Jacob's father, also passed,
At an old age, surrounded by his kin,
Jacob and Esau buried him at last,
And their family legacy did begin.

LINEAGE OF POWER

Generations of Edom, Esau's kin,
Born to him in Canaan, land of sin.
Wives from Canaan he took to bed,
Adah, Oholibamah and Basemath were wed.

Eliphaz from Adah was born,
Basemath bore Reuel, to whom he was fond.
Oholibamah's sons were Jeush, Jalam, and Korah,
All sons of Esau, as it says in Torah.

Esau's household grew too vast,
And his possessions no longer could last,
So he left for a land away,
Where he could flourish and his wealth display.

Esau lived in the hill country of Seir,
And was known by the name of Edom there.
These are the generations of his line,
The Edomites, as they're known in time.

Eliphaz's sons were chiefs of might,
Teman, Omar, Zepho, and Kenaz in sight.
Korah, Gatam, and Amalek were there,
Descendants of Eliphaz and Adah, a pair.

Reuel's sons were chiefs as well,
Nahath, Zerah, Shammah, and Mizzah did dwell,
In the land of Edom, Basemath's kin,
Descendants of Reuel, Esau's kin.

Oholibamah bore sons who became chiefs,
Jeush, Jalam, and Korah, the land's beliefs.
Esau's wife, Anah's granddaughter,
Their descendants prospered, the land they did conquer.

Seir the Horite's sons were Lotan, Shobal, Zibeon, Anah,
Dishon, Ezer, and Dishan, chiefs in Edom, a grandeur.
Lotan had a sister named Timna,
And Hemam was his son, this we find enigma.

Shobal's sons were Alvan, Manahath, and Ebal,
Shepho and Onam, five in total.
Zibeon's sons were Aiah and Anah the brave,
Found hot springs while his father's donkeys did crave.

Anah's children, Dishon and Oholibamah by name,
Hemdan, Eshban, Ithran, and Cheran, of Dishon's fame.
Ezer had sons Bilhan, Zaavan, and Akan,
Dishan had Uz and Aran, all with a plan.

The Horite chiefs were mighty and strong,
Lotan, Shobal, Zibeon, Anah, their reigns long.
Dishon, Ezer, and Dishan too,
All chiefs in the land of Seir, this we know to be true.

Before any king reigned over Israel's sons,
Kings of Edom ruled, one by one.
Bela, Jobab, Husham, and Hadad, we see,
Kings of Edom, mighty as can be.

JOSEPH'S COAT

Jacob lived in Canaan, his father's land,
Where he would tend his flock, with staff in hand.
Joseph, his favorite son, so bright and young,
Pastured the sheep with his brothers among.

But Joseph's dreams, so vivid and so bold,
His brothers hated, they were not consoled.
For in his visions, they would bow to him,
Their jealousy grew, their patience grew thin.

One day, while they were tending to the flock,
They saw Joseph coming, in envy they'd mock.
They plotted to kill him, to end his life,
And take his coat, the symbol of their strife.

But Reuben, eldest brother, had a plan,
To save Joseph, with a gentle hand.
He told them, "Throw him in the pit, not dead,
So we can sell him, and make coin instead."

And so they threw him in, alone and scared,
But then a caravan of Ishmaelites appeared.
They sold him for silver, twenty shekels to pay,
And Joseph was taken to Egypt that day.

Reuben came back, saw Joseph was gone,
He tore his clothes, the truth was now dawned.
They dipped Joseph's coat in goat's blood, so red,
And told their father, "Joseph's dead."

UNINTENDED ENCOUNTER

Judah left his kin to visit a friend,
Hirah, the Adullamite, whose name we comprehend.
In Adullam, he met a Canaanite daughter,
Shua was her name, and he took her as his lover.

Their union bore Er, their firstborn son,
And later Onan, a second one.
Lastly came Shelah, whose birthplace,
Was at Chezib, a familiar space.

Er was wicked and met his demise,
Leaving Tamar, his wife, in sorrowful cries.
Judah urged Onan to fulfill his duty,
To his late brother's wife, it was his responsibility.

But Onan refused, and wasted his seed,
And suffered the Lord's wrath indeed.
Judah then asked Tamar to remain,
A widow until Shelah's adulthood to sustain.

Time passed, and Shua's daughter had died,
So Judah mourned, and after, he decided,
To go and shear his sheep in Timnah,
With Hirah, his friend, a trusted comrade.

Tamar learned of Judah's plans,
To fulfill her desire, she hatched a plan.
She removed her widow's garments, covered her face,
And waited for Judah at the gateway of Enaim's place.

Thinking her to be a prostitute, Judah approached,
Offering her a young goat, he eagerly broached,
The idea of sexual relations with her.
Unknowing she was his daughter-in-law, as he whispered.

Tamar asked for a pledge, which he gave,
His seal, his cord, and staff, she took to save.
She conceived a child, and went on her way,
Putting on her widow's garments to not betray.

When Judah sent for the woman he sought,
His friend could not find her as he thought.
Judah avoided embarrassment and disgrace,
And let the matter rest, leaving without a trace.

Months later, Judah heard of Tamar's shame,
And demanded she be burned for her immoral game.
But she proved her innocence and revealed,
That he was the father, the truth now unsealed.

Judah recognized the items she had kept,
And acknowledged her righteousness, as he wept.
He had no further relations with her again,
As Tamar gave birth to twins, the story's end.

FALSELY ACCUSED

Joseph, sold into slavery,
Taken from his land to Egypt's shore,
Potiphar, a captain of the guard,
Bought him from the Ishmaelites' store.

But the Lord was with Joseph,
And he prospered in all he did,
Becoming his master's personal servant,
Overseeing all he owned, with no bid.

The Lord blessed Potiphar's house,
For Joseph's wisdom, grace, and might,
And he left Joseph in charge,
To care for all day and night.

But Potiphar's wife, with eyes on Joseph,
Sought his body and his soul,
But he refused her advances,
Saying, "I cannot commit this foul goal."

Day after day, she tempted him,
But he fled her sinful scheme,
Leaving his garment in her hand,
As he ran far away from her dream.

She called for help, lying and scheming,
Blaming Joseph for a lustful desire,
And Potiphar, hearing her tale,
Cast Joseph into prison, without any prior.

But even in his cell, Joseph thrived,
For the Lord was with him still,
Gaining favor with the prison warden,
And overseeing all with skill.

The Lord made all that Joseph did,
Prosper and thrive in his hand,
Despite his unjust imprisonment,
He continued to follow His command.

FATEFUL DREAMS

The cupbearer and the baker, both
Had angered Egypt's king, behold
In prison they were placed to wait
With Joseph, who kept watch and state

One morning they were filled with woe
And Joseph asked, "Why do you show
Such sadness on your faces now?"
"We've had a dream, but know not how

To understand what it might mean,"
They said, in hopes of help unseen
The cupbearer then spoke his dream
Of vines and grapes, it did seem

That he would soon be set free
And back to serving royalty
Joseph said, "Please think of me
When you regain your liberty"

The baker then did likewise tell
Of baskets filled with bread, as well
But in his dream, a darker fate
Awaited him, to his heart's hate

He'd be hung upon a post of wood
His flesh to be eaten, not so good
Pharaoh's birthday feast arrived
The dreams of both had been contrived

The cupbearer was set free to reign
But the baker was hanged in pain
And yet the cupbearer forgot
To mention Joseph, a sorry blot

PREPARATION IN TIMES OF PLENTY

Pharaoh stood by the Nile,
And in his dream, he saw
Seven cows, fat and fine,
Grazing on the marshy floor.

But then, seven other cows
Came up from the river too,
Thin and ugly, standing close,
To the fat cows they pursued.

The thin and ugly cows
Ate the fat cows, every one,
And then Pharaoh woke up
Before the dream was done.

He fell asleep again,
And in his dream, he saw
Seven ears of plump grain
Growing from a single straw.

But then, seven ears of grain
Came up, thin and scorched by wind,
And the thin ears swallowed whole
The plump ears, with no rescind.

When Pharaoh woke once more,
He knew his spirit was troubled,
So he called his priests and wise men
To interpret his dreams, if they were able.

But no one there could say
What the dreams might indicate,
Until the chief cupbearer spoke up
And told of a youth who could translate.

This Hebrew youth was brought forth,
And he heard Pharaoh's dream that day,
He said, "God will give an answer
For Pharaoh's good in every way."

The seven fat cows and the seven ears
Of good grain, they represented years,
Seven years of abundance, so it seems,
To be followed by famine and lean.

The thin cows and the thin ears
Represented famine and tears,
Seven years of scarcity and loss,
With hunger and poverty as the cost.

So Pharaoh took action, wise and true,
He appointed a man to see Egypt through,
And in the years of abundance, he did command
A fifth of the produce be stored at hand.

So when famine came to the land,
Egypt had plenty to withstand,
And through the youth's interpretation
They had secured a future, with no hesitation.

FACING FAMINE

Jacob sees the famine,
And says to his sons,
â€œWhy stare at each other in vain?
In Egypt, there's grain.â€

So they go to the land,
To buy what they need.
But Benjamin, he stays behind,
For Jacob fears he'll be confined.

Joseph was the ruler,
Selling grain to all.
His brothers came and bowed to him,
Their faces to the ground.

He knew them, but disguised himself,
And spoke harshly, accusing.
They denied his claims of spying,
But Joseph didn't believe them.

He demanded to see their youngest brother,
Before he'd let them leave.
He put them in prison for three days,
And Simeon, he did seize.

On the third day, Joseph spoke,
"Leave one behind to stay.
Go home and bring your youngest brother,
So that I may know you're honest and not spies.

They left with their bags of grain,
But found their money inside.
They were afraid of what God had done,
And told Jacob everything that had transpired.

So they planned to return,
With Benjamin by their side.
They hoped to prove their innocence,
And to regain their lost pride.

HIDDEN IDENTITY

Famine struck the land, a curse severe,
Egypt's grain they ate, their father did fear,
"Go back and buy more," he said with a sigh,
But they needed Benjamin to return, or else deny.

Judah spoke up, with conviction he pled,
"Send the boy with us, we'll bring him back," he said.
Their father was upset, he did not agree,
"Why did you tell him of Benjamin?" he queried.

"The man asked us," they said in defense,
"We didn't know it would lead to such consequence."
But Judah promised to keep the boy safe,
He would take responsibility and face any fate.

Their father agreed, but with gifts to bring,
A little balsam, honey, and other things,
They journeyed to Egypt with double the money,
And prayed for compassion, so their trip would be sunny.

Joseph saw Benjamin and his heart did stir,
He invited them to dine and began to confer,
They feared the worst, but Joseph had a plan,
He embraced them with kindness and did understand.

He asked of their father, and they replied,
"He's alive and well," with heads bowed they complied,
Joseph wept at the sight of his kin,
He composed himself and invited them in.

They dined in groups, as was the custom,
For the Egyptians would not eat with them,
But Joseph showed them love, though they were apart,
And they left with full bellies and a joyful heart.

THE SILVER CUP

In Egypt's land, so far away,
Joseph commanded his steward that day,
"Fill up the sacks with all they can carry,
And each man's money in his sack, tarry not, be merry.

Put my silver cup in the youngest's hold,
Along with his money for the grain so bold."
And so the steward did as he was told,
And the men set off with their donkeys, so bold.

But not far out, Joseph's voice did ring,
"Follow those men and their sacks, bring
My silver cup they've dared to steal,
And with words of grief, make them feel."

The men protested and denied their guilt,
Their innocence they swore was built,
But the cup was found in the youngest's sack,
And with sorrowful cries, they headed back.

To Joseph's house, they fell to the ground,
Judah and his brothers, in grief profound,
And Joseph asked, "Why this deed you've done?
You know I can divine, I am like none."

Judah begged for mercy and explained their plight,
Of their father's love for the youngest in sight,
And how they could not leave him behind,
Or their father's sorrow would be unkind.

In the end, Joseph showed them grace,
The guilty one would be his slave, face to face,
But the others could go in peace, so kind,
To their father, with a heavy heart in mind.

REMORSE AND RECONCILIATION

Joseph couldn't hold back his tears,
As he revealed himself to his peers,
"Leave me," he cried, "I need to speak,
With my brothers alone, so don't peak."

The Egyptians heard his sobs and cries,
As Joseph wiped the tears from his eyes,
He said to his brothers, "I am Joseph, your kin,
Is our father still alive within?"

His brothers were stunned and filled with fear,
They couldn't speak, their hearts were unclear,
Joseph said, "Do not be sad or sore,
God sent me to Egypt for something more."

"For five more years, famine will spread,
But God sent me ahead,
To save our lives and keep us fed,
And ensure that a remnant would be led."

"It wasn't you who sent me here,
It was God who brought me near,
And made me lord over Egypt's land,
With power and wealth at my command."

One by one, Joseph held them tight,
Shared his plans through the night.
"Go to our father, without delay,
Goshen awaits, there we'll stay."

Pharaoh was pleased to hear the news,
That Joseph's brothers had come to choose,
The best of Egypt's land to call their own,
And to prosper until the famine was gone.

Joseph sent them on their way,
With wagons and provisions for the day,
To their father Jacob, they made their plea,
"Joseph lives! He rules, come and see!"

Jacob, doubtful, couldn't conceive,
Till wagons of relief made him believe,
His spirit soared with joy and pride,
"I'll meet my son before I die," he cried.

SEVENTY SOULS

Israel's journey was long and hard,
With all he had, he traveled far.
To Beersheba, he made his way,
And offered sacrifices to God that day.

In visions of the night, God spoke,
Calling Jacob by name, his heart awoke.
"I am God," He said, "of your father true,
Fear not, for in Egypt, great things await you."

"I'll make you into a mighty nation,
And go with you to that foreign location.
I'll bring you back, and Joseph will be near,
To close your eyes when your end is near."

Jacob and his descendants, all,
Left Beersheba, answering God's call.
They traveled with wagons sent by Pharaoh's care,
With little ones, wives, and livestock rare.

The sons of Israel, Jacob's kin,
All traveled to Egypt, not leaving one behind.
Reuben, Simeon, and Levi too,
Judah, Dan, and Naphtali, to name a few.

All were there, every son and daughter,
Rachel's two, Benjamin and Joseph, the brothers.
And Bilhah's seven and Zilpah's sixteen,
In all, they numbered seventy, a mighty team.

Jacob sent Judah ahead to guide,
To Goshen, where Joseph would reside.
Joseph prepared his chariot, went to meet his dad,
And upon seeing him, wept, for he was glad.

Jacob said, "Now let me die, for I've seen your face,
And know you're alive, in this unfamiliar place."
Joseph went to Pharaoh, his family's story to tell,
That they were shepherds, their occupation, he would sell.

For in Goshen, they would dwell,
Where shepherds were not looked upon well.
And there, they would live in peace,
As God's chosen people, His love would not cease.

JOSEPH'S PLAN

Joseph spoke to Pharaoh of his kin,
"My father, brothers and flocks within
Canaan's land they've left behind,
And now in Goshen they hope to find

A place to live and graze their sheep,
For in Canaan famine's grip is deep."
Pharaoh asked the brothers' trade,
To which they said, "We're shepherds made,

As were our fathers, through the years.
We've come to Egypt, seeking gears
Of life to survive this drought,
We ask to live in Goshen, no more to scout."

Pharaoh then spoke to Joseph with care,
"Your kin have come, it's only fair
To grant them Egypt's best land to stay.
If any men are skilled, I may.

Employ them to care for my herd,
Let your family settle, let my word be heard."
Joseph brought his father Jacob to meet
Pharaoh, Jacob blessed the royal seat.

Pharaoh asked, "How old are you, sir?"
Jacob replied, "130, it's a blur,
Years of pain and difficulty,
Fewer than my fathers' longevity."

Jacob blessed Pharaoh once more,
And then he left his presence's shore.
Joseph gave his kin land and property,
In Rameses, Egypt's finest commodity.

He provided them with food to survive,
And supported them to help them thrive.
The famine was severe, it affected all,
In Egypt and Canaan, the land did fall.

Joseph sold grain in exchange for wealth,
To Egypt and Canaan, helping their health.
When the money was gone, the people cried,
"Give us fo.od, so we won't have died."

Joseph said, "Give your livestock to me,
In exchange, I'll give you food to eat."
They agreed, and Joseph took charge,
Exchanging food for their animals at large.

At the end of the year, they came again,
Saying, "All our money is spent, my friend."
Joseph bought all the land in Egypt's nation,
For Pharaoh, to help with starvation.

The people moved to the cities to live,
Their land and possessions, they did give.
Except for the priests, who had an allotment,
They didn't sell their land, it was a requirement.

Joseph gave the people seeds to sow,
And told them, "At harvest, a fifth you'll owe
Pharaoh, and the rest will be yours to keep,
For food and seeds, and the ones you keep."

The people thanked Joseph and Pharaoh too,
"Your kindness has saved us, and we'll serve you."
Israel lived in Goshen and acquired land,
And became fruitful, God's gracious hand.

Jacob lived for seventeen years more,
His life was blessed, to God he did adore.
The story of Joseph and his family's fate
Is one of God's mercy, it's never too late.

A PATRIARCH'S FAREWELL

Joseph's father was sick, he was told
So he took his sons, to his father he strolled
Jacob, his father, heard the news
He collected his strength and sat up, no time to lose

Jacob spoke of the blessings he received
From God Almighty, who he believed
And said his grandsons were now his
Like Reuben and Simeon, they too would be his

Israel's eyes were dim, he couldn't see
But Joseph brought the boys, close to be
Kissed and embraced, Israel was elated
He never thought this day could be fated

Israel blessed the boys in the Lord's name
And asked that his name would live on in fame
May they grow and prosper in the land
With Abraham and Isaac's name at hand

Joseph saw that his father's right hand
Was on the head of the younger, it was unplanned
He asked for it to be moved, for the firstborn's sake
But Israel knew what blessings to make

The younger, Ephraim, would be greater still
His descendants would multiply and fulfill
Israel's last wish before he died
God be with Joseph, bring him back to his side

And as a final gift to Joseph he gave
One portion more, from the land he saved
With sword and bow, from the Amorite's hand
May God bless Joseph's future, in his promised land.

TWELVE TRIBES OF ISRAEL

Jacob called his sons, to them he spoke,
To share the future that he foresaw, invoked.
"Listen to me," he said, "sons of Jacob,
Hear your father, Israel, speak and unlock.

Reuben, my firstborn, mighty and strong,
But your uncontrollable nature did me wrong.
You defiled my bed, and caused me shame,
Preeminence you won't have, such is your claim.

Simeon and Levi, brothers of might,
Their swords bring violence, a fearsome sight.
May my soul never join their council of wrath,
Their anger and self-will bring ruin and aftermath.

Judah, my son, a lion's cub you are,
From prey you've emerged, and have gone far.
As a lion, you crouch and lie in wait,
None dare stir you, for your power is great.

Your brothers will bow down, enemies tremble,
The scepter shall remain, till Shiloh assemble.
The obedience of people, to him it belongs,
From Judah's line, shall come the mightiest thrones.

Zebulun, your home will be by the sea,
A harbor for ships, your destiny to be.
Issachar, a strong donkey, between the folds he lies,
Bowed to carry burdens, a slave at forced labor tries.

Dan, one of the tribes of Israel, shall judge,
A serpent in the way, a horned viper's nudge.
Gad, attacked by raiders, fights at their heels,
Asher's food is rich, he yields royal meals.

Naphtali, a doe, let loose and free,
Utters beautiful words, his voice pure as can be.
Joseph, fruitful and blessed, a branch by a spring,
Over the wall, his branches hang, a sight to bring.

Though archers provoked, his bow remained firm,
From the hands of the Mighty One, his power did confirm.
Benjamin, a ravenous wolf, devours prey,
Dividing spoils in the evening, at the end of the day.

These are the twelve tribes of Israel, a sacred clan,
Jacob's blessing upon each, a unique plan.
Jacob passed away, to be with his kin,
Bury me with my fathers, in the field of Ephron, he did begin.

The cave in Machpelah, where his ancestors lay,
Abraham and Sarah, Isaac and Rebekah, Leah to stay.
The field purchased from the sons of Heth,
Jacob drew his feet, his last breath, in death he met.

JOSEPH'S TEARS

Joseph wept as his father passed
And called for physicians to embalm him fast
For forty days they worked to prepare
Such is the time required, they were aware

The Egyptians wept for seventy days
As they mourned the passing of Israel's ways
When mourning had ended, Joseph spoke
To Pharaoh's household, thus he broke:

"My father made me swear to bury him
In Canaan, where his grave was to begin
Please let me go and fulfill his request
Then I will return, my duties addressed"

Pharaoh granted his request to depart
And Joseph's family and servants made a start
They left behind their little ones and herds
And traveled to Canaan with a great many words

They stopped at the threshing floor of Atad
And mourned with sorrow, for Israel they had
For seven days, Joseph observed
His father's passing, as they all deserved

The Canaanites saw the mourning and said
"This is a grievous mourning for the Egyptians, it's led
To Abel-mizraim, named in this place
Beyond the Jordan, for Israel's embrace"

As Israel had commanded, his sons
Buried him in Machpelah, where it was done
Joseph returned to Egypt with his kin
And life continued, though they mourned within

When Joseph's brothers feared his wrath
They sent a message, clearing their path
As their father had commanded, they pled
For Joseph's forgiveness, so they wouldn't be dead

Joseph wept as he heard their plea
And forgave them, as they could see
He promised to care for them and their own
And to never hold their past against them alone

As time passed, Joseph saw the third generation
And knew his own death was nearing its station
But he was comforted, for God had a plan
To take care of his family, as He began

Joseph made the sons of Israel swear
To carry his bones from Egypt's lair
And though he died, embalmed, in a coffin
His legacy lived on, never to be forgotten.

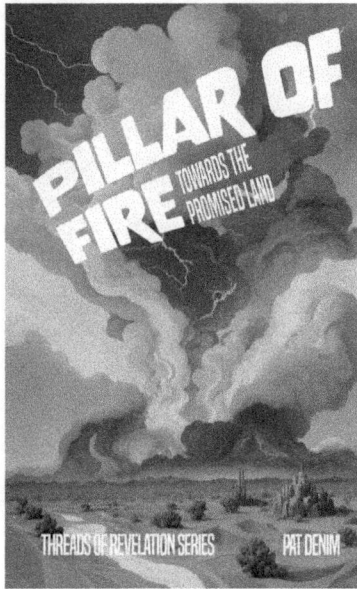

Next in the
Threads of Revelation Series:

Pillar of Fire:
Toward the Promised Land

Hi. I hope you have enjoyed this book. If you have a moment to spare, I would greatly appreciate it if you could take the time to review it.

If you gained valuable insights, or if your spiritual journey was influenced in any way, I would love to hear about it. Your opinion matters to me and I would be grateful if you could share your experience and thoughts by leaving a review.

www.ingramcontent.com/pod-product-compliance
Lightning Source LLC
Chambersburg PA
CBHW061748020426
42331CB00006B/1400